CREATURES PECULIAR
AND CROOKS

CREATURES PECULIAR AND CROOKS

Poems and Drawings by
Bain Mattox

Creatures Peculiar and Crooks
Copyright © 2017
by Bain Mattox

All rights reserved. All characters featured in this work of fiction and the distinctive names and likenesses thereof, and all related indicia are properties of Bain Mattox. No similarity between the names, characters, persons, or institutions, and any such actual entities is intended, and any such similarity which may exist is purely coincidental.

No portion of this book may be reproduced by any means without the express written consent of the copyright holder, except brief passages used in connection with a review.

For advertising, licensing, orders, or other inquiries, please visit www.garbagefactory.com

The Garbage Factory
Athens, Georgia, USA

If you are unable to order this book from your local bookseller, you may order directly from the publisher. Visit www.garbagefactory.com or www.bainmattox.net for contact information.

ISBN 978-0-9975227-5-4
10 9 8 7 6 5 4 3 2 1

IF YOU LOST SOMETHING, TRY LOOKING HERE

CREATURES PECULIAR AND CROOKS...................................1
THE APE ORF DOZEN 2
THE BOTHERSOME CALICO WEEVILY SNOOPS...........................4
CRAVEN THE CROOK...7
PTER..12
THE LAST CHAPTER GHOST..16
THE FACES...20
SUBSTITUTE CREATURE...22
THERE'S A MONSTER EATING THIS POEM 27
TINY TALL TINY TALL...28
TED, THE FOLDING CHAIR 29
SEVEN HAIKU..32
CAPTAIN BEEZOO, PART TWO.....................................36
THE MAN IN BLACK 40

CREATURES PECULIAR AND CROOKS

Creatures peculiar and crooks
Haunting the pages of books
Are born from the night
A lit match, candlelight
Create shadows from the gobbledygook

From these hideouts whence they come
They grumble and rumble and hum
From the corners of eyes
They slither and rise
From the crevices, dust and crumbs

But your comfort should well be restored
'Cause my pen is a mighty sword
That banishes them to paper,
To their sagas and capers,
Because I am their overlord

I trap them inside storybooks
And don them with less threatening looks
And I'll make them behave
And I'll keep you unscathed
From these Creatures Peculiar and Crooks.

THE APE ORF DOZEN

When all is lost and you don't know why
You've searched for things you cannot find
Everything's missing, it has to be somethin'
I'll tell you why ...
It's the Ape Orf Dozen

They flex their muscles, they lock their jaws
They clench their teeth, they sink their claws
Your ears will ring from their buzzin'
All is askew ...
From the Ape Orf Dozen

Their fur it stinks, from their head to their toeses
Big beady eyes lay on top of their noses
Dust clouds explode when their fur starts a fuzzin'
It's a ghastly sight ...
The Ape Orf Dozen

They clamour in packs, like wolves and dogs
Crawling out from their steamy bogs
Some of them brothers, some of them cousins
A nasty family...
The Ape Orf Dozen

They find something awesome and make it terrible
They take something pleasant and make it unbearable
They take things out, from where they was in
And never replacing them ...
They Ape Orf Dozen

Their bogs are filled up like a Lost and Found
Single shoes and jackets piled in a mound
Covered in filth and grime and be-scuzzened
They leave you in lurches ...
The Ape Orf Dozen

So when you can't find the things you can't find
You've retraced your steps, you've wracked your mind
You're making excuses, you're mother is fussin'
'Twas the ever-havoc-wreaking ... Ape Orf Dozen

THE BOTHERSOME CALICO WEEVILY SNOOPS

Scientists have done some new discovering
A force of nature that's always been hovering
But too small to see to the naked eye
These crafty critters ... identified

You know that feeling when clothes don't fit?
You can't seem to put your finger on it
All day you wiggle to make it feel right
Your pants feel too loose, but also too tight

Your shoes feel like there's sand in the bottom
Stray hairs in your shirt, but you can't seem to spot 'em
Your socks feel like they've got bubbly toes
Shoelaces too short to tie in a bow

That mysterious nuisance has finally been solved
An animal's all along been involved
And it is to blame for your clothing's distresses
Destroying your shoes, your socks, your dresses

When you're asleep, they crawl in your drawers
They sneak through the cracks in your closets' doors
Tightening threads and some they let out
Loosening hems all throughout

Some go outside and bring in some dirt
And carefully place it inside your shirt
Positioning hairs in nooks and crannies
In parts of your pants that tickle your fannies

They draw out your socks but only a little
An irritant that sets your toes to wiggle
Grains of sand they put in the cracks
That itch at your bum in the seams of your slacks

They stretch out the button holes almost twofold
So now all the buttons are too small to hold
They're friends with moths and invite them in
To nibble some holes in your wool cardigan

When you awake and start to get dressed
These out-of-sight devils are at rest in their nest
Leaving the mess of your garb and apparel
Making you dance, wild and feral

In their analysis, the scientists wanted to know
The reason these beasties bungled your clothes
They found that it's just like why ants makes their hills
Or bees make honey, and why termites drill

The bugs they are feeding off static 'lectricity
Pulling and pawing the nitty, the gritty
Charging up fabric to get themselves fed
Working the grindstone while you are in bed

So really these insects, they mean you no harm
They have no intent to cause itchy arms
The job that they do is not against you
But simply the work they must carry through

Garment malfunctions that make you feel irked
Are caused by a tribe that quietly lurks
Discovered and named by the scientist troop
As the "Bothersome Calico Weevily Snoops."

CRAVEN THE CROOK

Craven the Crook swoops like a rook
and steals from shops unexpecting
He sneaks in at night, when no one's in sight
And begins his devious collecting

He steals all the cash, and all of the stash
And cleans out the money completely
Leaving the businesses, nobody witnesses
Him slinking out so discretely

He goes town to town, a shadowy clown
Dressed head to toe in all black
Creeps from the dimness, with cat-like primness
Swipes and stuffs up his sack

Once, after a heist, his cravings enticed,
He noticed a quaint donut shop
A line out the door, he went to explore
his next loot-snatching stop

He watched the baristas, hands over fist-a-s
Collecting the cold hard cash
Donuts and bagels, coffees on tables
He'd loot and be gone in a flash

He waited 'til morning, when everyone's snoring
Too early for all to awake
Picked the lock by the loading dock
And slithered inside like a snake

He crept through the dark, a camouflaged shark
seeking out his prey
Approaching the till, he called on his skills
Prying open the tray

Just as he was grabbing, starting-to nabbing
Transferring bucks to his duffel
The donut shop lights flickered on bright
And faint sounds of someone's feet shuffled

Craven moved quick and dropped to the bricks
Crept into one of the dimly lit niches
The workers clocked in, began to begin
Brewing coffee and preparing the dishes

He rose to his feet, and tip-toed to meet
The workers that he had to thieve
His hand made a shape, with his coat that he draped
The shape of a gun up his sleeve

"This is a stick up, you'd best put your mitts up."
He said in a gravelly roar
The workers they spun; a man with a "gun"
Was standing there right in their door!

He tied up their arms, not meaning them harm
And sat them all down on the floor
He gagged up their mouths, to quiet their shouts
When suddenly, ajar was the door!

A sleepy-eyed patron, a babe-holding matron
Approached the confused Mr. Craven
She ordered a coffee, a donut with toffee
Shocked was the robbing black raven

He looked all around, up and then down
And grabbed a freshly brewed pot
Filling up a mug, this jittery thug
Placed the donut in the hand of the tot

The mom gave him dollars, he sweated his collar
Hoping the jig wasn't up
He opened the drawer, One more time more-er
And she put a tip in the tip cup

The door swung again, another walked in
And another, another, a-nother
A line-up had formed, right out the door
And Craven wanted his mother

He spent the next hour slinging the flour
And coffees and pastries and juice
He collected the funds, the neatly stacked ones
And served the front of the line to caboose

Craven, surprised, was having a time
That he found he really enjoyed
Smiles on faces, and customers' graces
And feeling like he was employed

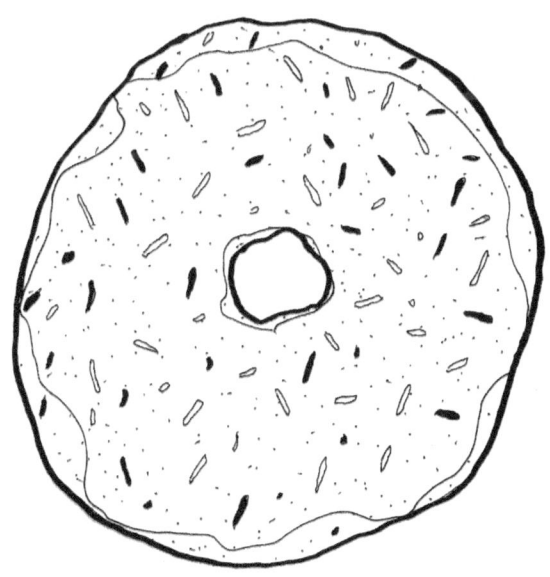

The line died down, and he hadn't drowned
He felt pleased with pleasing the pop
And then they walked in, a pair of twins
Two boys in blue, two cops

The officers entered, and walked to the center
Craven stood there in a tizzy
"A dozen, to go," one said really slow
And Craven began to feel dizzy

He gathered the donuts, tried not to go nuts
with worry and fear he'd been caught
The box he held out, to the two who stood stout
But he froze there right on the spot

Are you alright? One cop said outright
Craven with sweat on his face
Unable to speak, his foot it squeaked
And he ran right out of the place

The cops were confused, but they put two and two
Together when they found the clerks
They untied the ropes, and helped them cope
With the mishap of the thief's handiwork

Craven, long gone, safe from hereon
Escaping the close-call arrest
He'd only got away with the donut tray
That he ate with his mind at rest

This shadowy rover, now a couple towns over
Miles from the donut shop caper
roamed through the town, eyes to the ground
Which is where he saw a newspaper

A classified ad read, in bold letters it said
"Now Hiring Donut Shop Clerk"
He got so excited, and simply delighted
He'd really been missing the work

The shop was nearby, he went to apply
The case filled with goodies and tarts
He shook the hand of the donut shop man
And the man said, "When can you start?"

That was the day, that Craven will say
was the turning over of a new leaf
He serves the coffee and donuts with toffee
And no longer's a no-good thief.

PTER

Pter lost an "E" from his name
He doesn't know where it went
He checked the dresser, the cupboard, the pantry
Even the dryer vent

Pter peeked under his armpits
He checked between his toes
Under his chin, over his shoulder
Maybe it's up his nose?

Pter opened all the boxes
Backgammon, checkers, and chess
He scattered the jacks, rolled the dice
Still with no success

Pter poured the cereal out
He ran the milk through a strainer
Spooned the mayo, squirted the mustard
He emptied all the containers

Pter scoured the blades of grass
He needled through the hay
Upturned the stones, dug through the dirt
He kneaded through the clay

Pter unrolled the toilet paper
Unclogged the bath-tub drain
He lifted the lid, examined the bowl
And plugged his nose with disdain

Pter crawled up under his bed
Turned down his blankets and sheets
He rifled his desk, un-hung the hangers
Unlaced his boots and cleats

Pter spotted the shelf in the corner
Filled with books and mags
He leafed through pages, he licked his fingers
And sifted through the rags

Through Pter's perusal: "Eureka, I've got it!"
He remembered the book by his bed
He borrowed his "E" to bookmark a page
When he read all he had read

Pter opened the book... THERE IT WAS!
Marking his very next chapter
He replaced the "E"; his name was complete
Peter lived happily ever after.

MILDRED THE MIGGLE

Mildred the Miggle
Snorts when she giggles
'Specially when you tickle her belly
She's also quite ticklish
On her toes that look picklish
And like most toes, hers are quite smelly

Oh wait. What's a Miggle?
Well, it's right in the middle
of a Queen and a Ghost and a Duck
And I'll try to describe
How these things they collide
Here it goes, so please wish me luck....

She floats around town
In what looks like a gown
But it's feathers from her head past her knees
And her gown appears regal
When she flies like an eagle
And she flaps her duck-wings with great ease

On her head is a crown
Built in, fastened down
I know all of this seems preposterous
The crown isn't gold
But it's weathered and old
Like a horn from a wild rhinoceros

Her garb aforementioned
Is from another dimension
Opaque and in the shape of a ghost
Round at its crest
Like a tattered old dress
Flows by her shins southernmost

Her eyes black and beady
Look sesame-seedy
Below them a yellowish bill
And she lets out a quack
When she's hungry for snacks
And throws loaves of bread on the grill

She's noble and kind
With charity in mind
And she works at the cotton exchange
She greets all the buyers
Gets them their desires
Despite her looks, no one acts strange

She punches her clock
And walks to the dock
Spreads her duck-wings and takes flight
Over the water
She waves to the otters
On her commute home for the night

She opens her door
To her flat on her floor
And tosses her mail on her couch
Her roommate is home
Watching TV alone
She says Hi to Howby the Houch

Oh wait. What's a Houch?
It's a Pig with a Pouch
With fur made of leaves like a Shrub
Well, that's an odd story
A new territory
So the two sit, relax and eat grub.

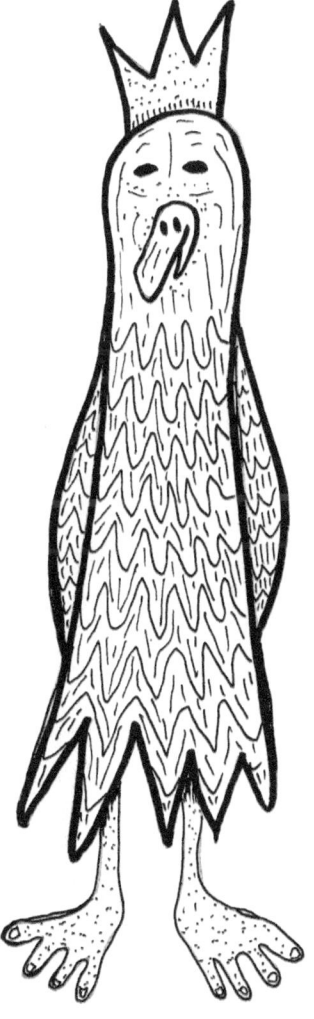

THE LAST CHAPTER GHOST

An elderly man reads in his den
Reading a book and he's near to the end
The final chapter he'll read at first light
After he's rested his eyes for the night

The man climbs in bed, pulls up the quilt
Ready for sleep in this house that he built
The words of the chapters swirl in his head
"I'll finish tomorrow," he yawns as he says

His eyelids squeeze out the light of the lamps
The quiet and dreaminess strike up their dance
He gets to that floaty feeling of sleep
Right as one's body feels peacefully deep

He wakes in the morning and then gets a scare
His body's in bed, but he's standing there
His carcass is still, but he's very awake
He looks at his hands, and they're not quite opaque

He'd passed away during his slumber
He'd reached his final age's number
He stood there gazing at his body, now dead
The ghost of himself now stands by his bed

"Why's there no heaven, or whatever you call it?
I've given to charity from my own wallet
I've lived and I've loved, and I wanted Hereafter,"
But then he remembers that unread chapter

He reaches for the book, but his hands pass through it
His paper obsession, he wanted to view it
The touch he possessed to pick up and grab
Is something this ghost no longer had

The words in the book beckon and mock him
Marooned in his mansion, his ghostliness blocks him
From comfortably curling up and reading his novel
Alone and confused, he wept and he groveled

His spectral dilemma, and infinite time
He only can moan and wander and cry
The empty walls of where he was once living
Are cold, quiet, dark, unforgiving

***

The word got about, this man had logged-out
His lawyer to settle the will, no doubt
The man's son arrived to settle estates
To go through his things and cut through the tapes

The man watched as his offspring pored through effects
Albums of photos on which to reflect
He longed to reach out and touch that dear son
He wished he had hugged him more when he was young

A montage of memories in his mind played within
The one thing in common he shared with his kin
The length of the books, seemed to grow like the boy
Who always chose reading, versus playing with toys

The father would sit on Saturday morn
His son would sit reading on the living room floor
Calling out words that he didn't understand
And the father took pleasure in lending a hand

His heir, packing boxes, began to hum
A song that used to be sung by his mum
The ghost recognizing it, joined in the song
An ethereal duet, as they both sang along

Junior grew tired and sat on the bed
The one where his father had come to be dead
He reached for a book that laid on the night-stand
He picked it up and opened the book with his right-hand

The spectre sat right down beside him
And watched as his boy faintly supplied him
With the type-text right there in the book
Over his shoulder, the man over-looked

Pages kept turning, chapter uncoiled
Stories were told, villains were foiled
Finally, Chapter Fourteen filled the page
The boy and his father were hooked and engaged

In the same meter, their irises syncing
Tandemly reading, tandemly blinking
At last, that final page had arrived
They both reached the period at the very same time

Slowly the front and the back came to close
Trapping the words, the type, the prose
The novel was carefully put back in place
Right on the night stand, right by the vase

The two men stood and faced each other
The man gazed at eyes just like the boy's mother's
His son looking back but seeing thin air
Walked right through him, walked to the stairs

The man stood there by the bed in his room
He suddenly smelled a familiar perfume
A glitter of mist appeared right in front of him
His betrothed beauty, his late wife had come for him

He reached out a hand, and felt someone hold it
The warmth of the grip, as someone consoled it
He closed his eyes and let it lead him
Into the hereafter that ultimately freed him

The last chapter ghost had now met his maker
He'd breathed his last breath, he'd walked his last acre
He stood there with dearly departed at hand
No longer a ghost, and no longer a man

**

Miles away from his parents' home
The son holds his daughter, all alone
He quietly hums the song he recalled
Watching her sleepily listen, enthralled

He thinks of the tale that he read on the bed
But it wasn't the story that danced in his head
He felt a completion, a job that was done
It was time with his father, and a father with son.

THE FACES

Have you ever noticed the faces?
They pop up in all sorts of, all kinds of places
The grains of the wood swirl into shapes
The creases of curtains, the folds in the drapes

I started naming the ones that I'd see
Like the man with the beard in the bark of the tree
Winston, I call him; I bet he is wise
Like one of those soothsayer, wizardy guys

There's also Claudette; she's the face in the curtains
The folds make her wrinkly face look so certain
Like she's keeping a secret she never will tell
Maybe her secret's a conjuring spell

Then there's the shadowy Gilbert at night
Who only shows up when you turn out the light
His goofy clown face projects on the wall
His ears are enormous, but his eyes are so small

The guy I call Jack, he's forever in wood
Droopy and down, but inherently good
The wood grains give him a lion-like mane
With a nose like a horse, his expression mundane

The swirls of the plaster ceiling straight up
Shape into a child holding a cup
Iris is sipping the same mug of tea
Forever up there, for just me to see

I sit there sending these faces my stare
I know that they're really not really there
But what if I also exist in their worlds?
My face in their grains, their folds, and their swirls.

SUBSTITUTE CREATURE

Come hear this tale of a horrible creature
Who hides in plain sight as a substitute teacher
He feeds off of children who cannot behave
On days when the real teacher's off for the day

He stands upright, just as tall as my dad is
His grimacing mouth smirks infinite sadness
His hideous claws are like that of a bear
But zig-zagged in scales instead of with hair

A Gargoyle's face sits plump on his neck
With boils and lumps and silvery flecks
His lizardy body oozes and goos
Clopping around on his goatishy hooves

Town to town, with purpose but sluggish
Drives his red truck with one piece of luggage
He seeks other second-hand teachers in vain
To fetter them up, and steal their names

Once he has kidnapped the perfect professor
He ransacks the house, the kitchen, the dresser
He finds the number for the schools close in reach
To let them know he's prepared to teach

He dresses each morning in a shirt and a tie
Brown pleated slacks and socks with stripes
Oozily slips on a mask that is man-like
And human-hand gloves that look human-hand like

Sits by a phone, in the little phone nook
In hopes that a teacher succumbed to the "gook"
Or maybe the flu or a doctor's appointment
Or an errand to pick up their foot-fungus ointment

The vibrating, jangling phone rings in place
The need for a teacher is always the case
He takes a deep breath and takes on his role
And dampens his grumbly voice of a troll

The gal on the line buzzes his ear
With promise of pay for the day for to rear
A classroom of pupils that patiently wait
To be lectured through their lessons today

The creature accepts, he drools on his chest
His hands rub together in hopes to digest
A bad little kiddie, that gets out of line
He'll capture and eat with a nice glass of wine

The funny thing is, he's really quite apt
At teaching the lessons and the chalk-talk of class
Another thing is, he really rejoices
Instilling the knowledge to all girls and boyses

If he is teaching, he doesn't feel hunger
It's like it's some kind of spell that he's under
But the moment a child gets vaguely troubley
His tummy juices get rumbly and bubbly

The creature he revels in kids' bad behavior
He dreams about future flavors he'll savor
He'll choose one and ask them to stay after class
All pleasing meals, lad or lass

So from this tall tale-y legend I've told you
I don't mean to scare or insult you or scold you
But next time a proxy's in place of your teacher
Be good, 'cause it might be the substitute creature.

ODDLY SHAPED MAN

Here's a story,
About an oddly shaped man
It won't be boring
I'll do the best that I can

Instead of round edges
His are all squared
Triangles and wedges
From his toes to his hair

All of his fingers
Look like icicles
Makes it hard for him
To ride bicycles

His face is flat on a head
That's a pyramid
His hair is crossed like the lines
On graph paper grids

Besides all of these parts,
He's got a heart-shaped heart
He's got a brain-shaped brain
And how you feel ... he feels the same

He rides a pony
To and from town
His pony's bony
And low to the ground

Over by the hedges
He met an angular girl
She shared his square edges
And her name, it was Pearl

One rectangle
Another rectangle
Icicle fingers
Now entangled

The oddly shaped mister
Found his missus
He slantingly kissed her
She slanted back the kisses

Besides all of these parts
They've got heart-shaped hearts
They've got brain-shaped brains
And how he feels ... she feels the same.

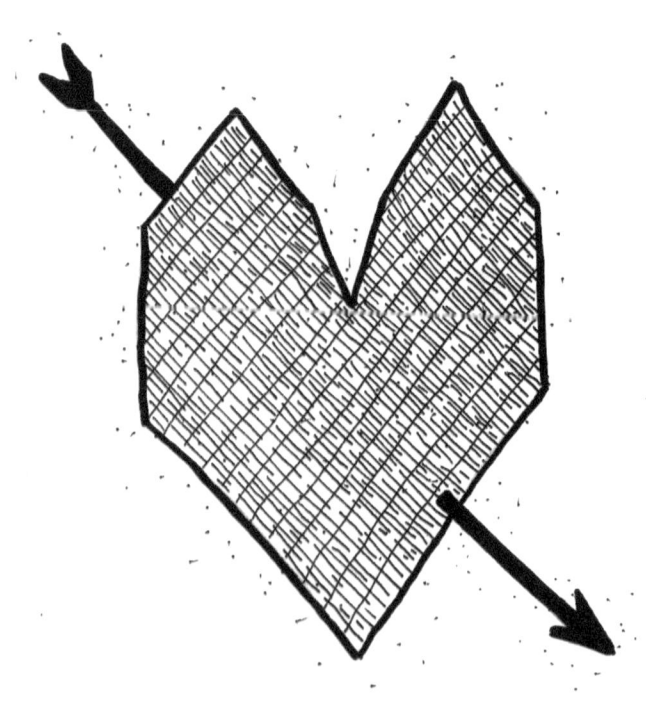

THERE'S A MONSTER EATING THIS POEM

If I were you, I'd run away
There's something scary, and we're it's prey
It feeds on words, and on us who read them
As I write this, the words are feeding him

Don't look down towards the end of this poem
It leaves a trail of slime below him
As he munches vowels and nouns
He crunches and slobbers all of them down

You better hurry and finish reading
Because he's gaining and starting-to speeding
Faster and faster he gobbles a lot
Each part of speech, each theme, each plot

Oh no! He just ate that metaphor
And that imagery's gone, right down his trap door
Insatiable beast that ingests all the letters
And adverbs and adjectives with no one to fetter

Oh Gosh! He's so close, don't look! run away!
His jowls approaching the last rhyming phrase
He'll skip over words and chew us to pulps
Too late! He's right here, Oh no!...

TINY TALL TINY TALL

A very tiny family had a very giant son
He was seven feet tall at the ripe age of one
He grew and grew taller than all the houses' chimneys
He ate giant plates of food but remained rather skinny

The son became a man, and fell in love and tied the knot
With a tiny little lady, at least to him, but to others not
She stood as high as a lampost, over corners of the street
Her head would block the sun from the others at her feet

The woman became a mother, and the man became a father
To a little tiny, teeny weeny, shrimpy mini-daughter
And she up grew into a girl and then into a lady
Never as tall as her daddy's toes, about as tall as a baby

The miniature woman met her mate, a lovely pint-sized man
And they'd go strolling after dinner, tiny hand in tiny hand
The couple became parents, and their hearts were filled with joy
On the day that she gave birth, it was a giant baby boy.

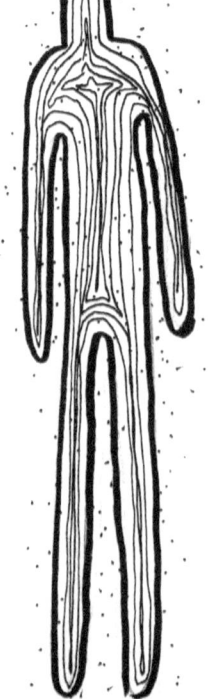

TED, THE FOLDING CHAIR

Hello, my name's Ted, and I'm a folding chair
I was born in a factory in the middle of nowhere
I rode on a train and a sixteen-wheeler
Delivered and sold to a folding chair dealer

Bought by a company that took me all over
To all sorts of parties, from Paris to Dover
Traveled the world, from bottom to top
Loading and unloading, starts and stops

A few of us got loaded into a church
Where we witnessed a celebration of birth
The priest took a tiny handful of water
And wet the red hair of someone's new daughter

The child seemed sort of weepy and bothered
But she was then comforted by her father
Who held her proudly amongst kin and friends
And stood in line to shake hands at the end

A new adventure: we were put in a tent
Facing a circle of mulch and cement
Children and families filed on in
Just in time for the lights to go dim

The girl with the cottony pink-colored candy
Sat on me, stood up, sitting and standing
Wiggled excitedly at the circusy show
The clowns and the animals wowing the rows

Another time I was set out at dawn
Right as the dew settled down on the lawn
Supporting a graduate robed in dark blue
She wore a cap, which she ultimately threw

She left me behind briefly, walked 'cross a stage
Right after someone had called out her name
She then returned with a rolled up paper
Tied with some ribbon, that she untied later

My favorite time, they lugged me in place
They draped all my comrades in satin and lace
The bride and groom kissed, both tall and lanky
The lady that sat on me weeped in her hanky

I felt so honored to be there that day
That two happy people decided to say,
"I do" and "I do," "Yes, let's be together
Forever and ever and ever and ever."

Occasions they came, occasions they went
Carted to all sorts of joyous events
I was an audience just like the people
Who used us in gardens and big tops and steeples

Oh what a joy to be a spectator
At weddings, affairs, and shindigs we catered
Sometimes I lucked out to be in front rows
Close as can be to grandiose shows

There was one time that sticks with me still
They drove us on up to a house on a hill
Where people in black clothing started to gather
Not looking happy, but looking much sadder

A red-headed woman chose me for her chair
Right in the front of this bitter affair
What kind of party does everyone cry?
It seems as though somebody has died

I felt a feeling so unlike before
The weight of the woman felt more like a chore
I did what I could to straighten on up
Supporting the woman who sat in a slump

I thought of the strawberry-headed child
Back at the chapel so meek, so mild
I thought of the girl with the cotton candy
Breathlessly watching the circus clowns dancing

That timid girl all draped in pride
Tossing her hat with her class that time
The kiss of a bride and groom embarking
On that curve of life that clearly was arcing

The coppery-crowned, weighed-down daughter
Who sat on me mourning the loss of her father
I was a place to sit all along
To take the load off, in between songs

I was there too, for these wonders momentous
Reinforcing from up under, a foldable apprentice
I had been blessed to watch this girl grow
Through her whole life and the times she has known

I was there, her folding chair
At all of the joyous and gorgeous affairs
And I'll be there then, with family and friends
For her to someday need me again.

SEVEN HAIKU

#1
Rollerskating squid
Finally saved up enough
For each tentacle

#2
If oranges had eyes
I'd probably not eat them
Regardless how hungry

#3
Dinosaur lawyer
Put a T-Rex in jail once
For stealing toothpaste

#4
Nesting Dolls can't love
The dolls don't have any hearts
Because they're empty

#5
Insects have grandads
They look the same but wrinkly
And also use canes

#6
My taco just spoke
But he didn't speak Spanish
He spoke Pig-Latin

#7
The clouds are swollen
Like a baby's full diaper
I hope it's not pee

DOCTOR REDBEARD

Doctor Redbeard is our family practitioner
Checks our heart beats with a stethoscope listener
Prescribes us our ointments
At our checkup appointments
And our ailments, he is the christener

But from the ripe age of ten-plus-three
Redbeard sailed the seven seas
Mopping the poop deck
And rummaging shipwrecks
On a pirate ship, for a pirate was he

He's now retired from that bootleg profession
'Cause his calling, his utmost obsession
Was healing the sick:
Vaccines, finger pricks,
So he ended his piracy session

Now, I'm not trying to be rude
But I feel his judgment is skewed
Because some of his cures
Are a little obscure
And seem to come from a pirate's-eye view....

Let me give you a case in point
My brother, he sprained his joint
So instead of a cast
Cannonball oil was passed
To my mother, to apply and anoint

Another time, Judy, my sister
Developed a nasty blister
He put forth a plan
To swap a hook for her hand,
That crazy retired pirate mister

My oldest big brother Titus
Had a bad case of Laryngitis
A talking parrot was prescribed
Who took crackers as bribes
So poor Titus wouldn't catch bronchitis

A slingshot accident occurred
And an eye got damaged and blurred
My poor brother Hatch
Was given an eye-patch
An injury an ice pack could cure

One time, he doctored my Mum
Who suffered from a sour tum
He gave her a map
And it warned her of traps
But led to a chest full of rum

I bonked heads with my sister Meg
I've got a bump that's the size of an egg
And now I'm afraid
That Redbeard will say
To switch out my head for a peg-leg.

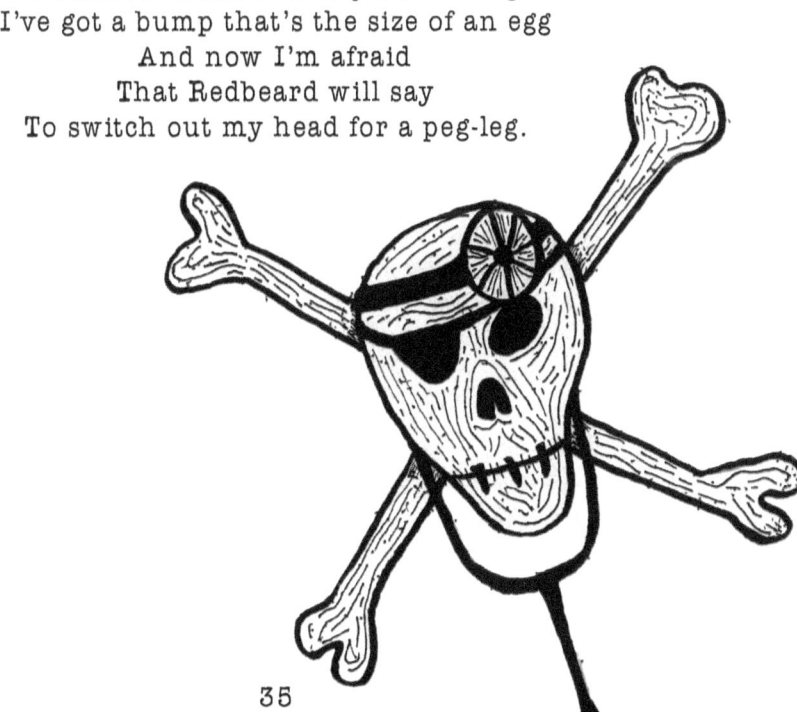

CAPTAIN BEEZOO, PART TWO

I'm Captain Beezo in my hot air balloo'
On my home to Kalamazoo
I made a wrong turn, last time I saw you
But now I'm in rou' back to Kalamazoo

I anchor my ship to the dock on the bay
I slide down the rope and I call the valet
He hands me a token that's made out of clay
For me to retrieve my balloo' from the bay

The grayish wood path is littered with gerbils
Their squeaking and squirming makes noises and burbles
Most of them speechless, but some of them verbal
The smell of my city is smoky and herbal

A telegram hangs on the door to my shack
Stuck to the wood with a golden thumb-tack
It's a note from a Hippogriff named Crackerjack
Who's hiring me to pick up his Cloud Almanac

A Cloud Almanac is a bible of news
With byways and flight paths for fowl to use
Scribed from the highest-flying bird's-eye view
It gives ones with wings, winged avenues

A quite simple request, but I lie down to rest
In my warm and inviting quaint little nest
I'll leave at first light, 'cause that'd be best
Before I head out, and back to the west

Arise from my hammock, I put on my knickers
Grab up my suitcase, all covered in stickers
Mementos from travels, stuck on the wicker
I extinguish the bedside candle that flickers

The Kalamazoo moon shared the sky with the sun
One setting, one rising, as my journey's begun
Triton, god of the sea, is out for a run
Through the mirrory waves, with his mermaid hon'

Off in the distance, I see constellations
Descending to join the day population
A lion, a warrior, and other formations
Stars turn to flesh, for the daytime duration

Further and further out over the water
I see Mrs. Hydra and her teenage daughter
Eighteen heads between them going in for the slaughter
Of a school of watermelons, swimming underwater

Venturing further, the center of the sea
Nessie from Loch Ness is swimming so free
"A long way from Scotland!" I call down to she
"I'm on vacation!" She yells back to me

Just a few moments later, I shout "LAND HO!"
It's seems kind of foolish, because I'm all alone
But nevertheless, where I am to go
Is forward in front of me, the Island of Yo

"The Island of Yo" it says on the pillar
This island is known for its pink caterpillars
The town's still asleep; I've not seen it stiller
I land in the wheat fields of island's wheat miller

There's a corner shop here, my reason for coming
That's run by a Yeti who's known for her humming
She accompanies her songs with a tempo-less drumming
She's really quite pleasant, and rather becoming

It's like she already knows, before I could look
That I've come for the Hippogriff's almanac book
Up on the highest shelf, she pulls from a nook
And from her hand, it's the book I took

So back to balloo', to stoke up the fire
But I stop to listen to a Banshee choir
High-pitched singing, accompanied by a lyre
Collecting coins for their busking in an old truck tire

I pass on my way a Cyclops curmudgeon
Who's the keeper of the island's jail and dungeon
A large chess king piece that he uses as a bludgeon
But he's using it currently to scratch at a bunion

And before I can blink, I'm off to the east
In tandem with a gaggle of miniature geese
Flying in a V, and dressed like police
Scanning the shoreline, and keeping the peace

Just down below, a ghost-ship sails
Carrying messages in bottles, and lost-letter mail
And its crew is quiet, foggy, and pale
And it vanishes at the sight of a breaching whale

As the sun starts to set, and the earth looks flat
The sky's littered with echo-locating bats
The moon fingernails in its dusk habitat
I speed up by turning the balloo's thermostat

And there she is, my city, my rock
My speed in time, has beaten the clock
A horde of birds, a resting flock
So many, the pelicans are in the shape of the dock

Again I throw the anchor to land
Home is awaiting this weary old man
Take my clay token from the valet's hand
Pass by the gerbils, away from the strand

I walk up the path to my whimsical shack
The Hippogriff's been waiting for me to get back
I hand him his cherished Cloud Almanac
Wrapped in a waterproof, walrus-skin sack

He emits a sound, like a reeded bassoon
And hands me a compass that belonged to the moon
It shows in-between directions that no-one's ever been to
Like the in-between notes, on a piano untuned

No better payment, or a gift yet to be
For a hot air balloo' captain such as me
I've trekked to the poles, I've voyaged the seas
I've globe-trotted, sea-fared, I'm a migratee

The sky's the limit, and thereon through
There's no place that I cannot go to
So I set my compass, and I board my balloo'
Now on to oblivion from Kalamazoo.

THE MAN IN BLACK

The autumn rain is beginning to wane and dripping from the trees
The sky is grizzled, a light mist drizzles and dampens all the leaves
My head is freezing, my nose is sneezing, my ears wind-tunnel chilly
I walk towards home, I assumed alone, the wet roads slick and hilly

Now I will say, to my dismay, I'm cursed with an absent mind
I misplace things -- my scarf, my keys -- which make things hard to find
Before my drifting, my hat went missing, so I just left without it
I cursed my name, for it's me to blame, and I've no doubt about it

Angrily, I walk through leaves, my head is left to suffer
Cold and wet, and I regret losing my nice, warm buffer
On top of that, the missing hat, I've also lost my umbrella
So here I am, a tortured sham; me, the forgetful fella

This early morning, most are snoring, sleeping through this drear
But I hear steps, as on I schlep, coming from the rear
Over my shoulder, I peer right over, and see someone in the distance
I turn around, my heart it pounds, from this creep's mere existence

I can see his eyes on me -- bulging bug-eyed staring
His face unkind, locked on mine, and me now he is scaring
Walking tall, his neck is shawled; he wears a long black slicker
His feet they shuffle, the leaves they ruffle, and I start walking quicker

I feel concern; I take a turn, in an attempt to lose him
But I look back; the Man in Black has turned and I still view him
I speed up my pace; my rain-soaked face drips also with sweat from fear
But he's maintaining, even gaining, now closer to my rear

He lets out a sound, as our feet hit the ground, but I keep running away
I can't comprehend him, no way to befriend him,
no want to be predator's prey
In my mind, the man behind is sputtering slurs and howls

I only imagine a slimy dragon, foaming from his jowls
Now I'm certain, my senses alertin', he's coming right after me
And so I bolt, in a jolt, so I can safely be free
I turn the street, with lightning feet, and spot my home's front door

I look back, and the Man in Black ... is not there anymore
I go inside, glad I'm alive, and lock the bolt behind me
I turn off the lights, in such a fright, praying he won't find me
I go upstairs, rather scared, and peep out through the drapes

The Man in Black has found my shack, he's right outside my place
From his cloak, this grizzly bloke, takes some items out:
Pen and paper; huffing and puffing vapor, and writes something down
And just like that, the Man in Black,
leaves a bundle and stalks away down the street

And on my doormat, this black-cloaked bat has left
something behind for me
I sneak down the stairs, still rather scared, as slow as my feet will let me
Trying to decipher if that mean viper, is waiting to jump out and get me
I peek out the glass and see a wet mass of something that's made of yarn

A note set on top, right on my door stop -- I'm still quite fearful of harm
Against better judgment, my hand starts to budge it,
and opens the door to a crack
I glance outside, in case he still hides, that ominous man in black
My heart a hot torch, I look down at my porch,
inspecting the sopping wet gift

My breath leaves my lungs, and out drops my tongue,
as the cloud of fear, it lifts
That yarn-made slop with the note on top is in fact my hat for my head
I pick up the paper, and solved this caper,
'cause here's what his note had said,
"I don't mean to bother, I tried to holler, but this fell from your pocket
I followed you home, 'Cause you seemed to not know
that you in fact had dropped it."

www.ingramcontent.com/pod-product-compliance
Lightning Source LLC
Chambersburg PA
CBHW020625300426
44113CB00007B/786